Living
with
Alzheimer's

A
Poetic
Expression

Margaret Barnes Carter

DEDICATION

This book is dedicated to all those who are on the journey through Alzheimer's and to those who are helping them along the way. We cannot take this journey without loved ones to support and help us.

I am fortunate to have strong support. My husband, Roscoe Owen Carter III has from the very beginning of this journey been at my side. He is my knight in shining armor who helps me remember, guides me and loves me as I am. I could not go on this journey without him. My daughter, Janet Carter, is also my support who understands on a deep level what it means to "live" with Alzheimer's. She is the one who has made it possible to turn my desire to share my poems about a journey with Alzheimer's into reality. My two sons, Matthew Owen Carter and Paul Joseph Carter are also my staunch advocates and supporters.

This book is also dedicated to those in my family who walked this same path, but without the understanding and care that is now available: my father, his mother, and many others.

CONTENTS

PART I

Where Poems Are Born

Deep inside on a cellular level
Poems are born.
At first, a fleeting flash,
A gently tickle, a whisper.

The whisper grows, shaped into words.
Words collide and mature into strings
Then strings to stanzas
And come alive.

Only then can the mind
Shape words into structure
For others to see and share
And perhaps to grow.

But, calamity often occurs
And whispers die
Before being brought to life
Leaving nothing behind.

Poetry is giving voice
To emotions, to feelings, to visions;
Uncovering the souls
Of thoughts and words.

Poetry flows through our veins
And warms or chills us
Letting us see the world anew
And opens our hearts to others.

The Unraveling

I am unraveling from whom I was
To some new being with
Threads breaking and
Connections unconnecting.
I feel
Isolated,
Unrelated,
Separated.
What can hold me together
Other than skin and bone:
Remembrance of my earlier me,
Love's connections to others,
Acceptance of who I am
And who I will come to be.
This I can live with.

Blue Sky Oceans

Archipelagos of white
Sail slowly across
The blue sky ocean
Until the sheer winds
Break them asunder.
Sumatra saunters southward
As the Canary's
Push from Africa
And the Aleutians
Drift slowly westward.
If I could climb aboard
I'd sail away with them
And leave behind all grief,
But love is here on earth
And here I will remain.

Face Talks

A lift of brow
A tilt of head
A sideways glance
A whispered frown;
With slitted eyes
And stifled sigh
We speak volumes
Without a word.

Mirror Neurons

I see with my ears
And hear with my eyes.
I taste other's loss
And smell their deep fear.

Sorrow masked behind a smiling face,
Loneliness cloaked with droop of shoulder,
Hatred hidden in a twist of phrase:
Emotions jumbled and out of place.

Mirror neurons that unlock the earth
And unmask deeply buried deceit
Leaving space for all to grow anew
Rising triumphant from new birth.

Little Dots of Darkness Fall Upon the Ground

Little dots of darkness fall upon the ground.

First a sprinkle covering the land black dot by black dot with nothingness in its place.

Slowly first, 'til spreading dots forms black holes in the landscape, lacey patterns with spidery connections holding the land together.

Hills pockmarked.

Trees in shreds.

Sweet meadows pocked with holes.

Dots rain down and gather in the low places.

When enough, they run in black rivers
Changing, life giving, cool streams
To black anaerobic pools of nothingness.

Even in the Midst

Even in the midst of
Lostness and disconnection,
I seek pathways.

Even in the depths of night
With no moon nor stars,
I see glimmers of light.

Even in the barren desert
Covered with parched sand
I search for sweet water.

Even in swirling chaos
Filled with disorder,
I sift for meaning.

In the Depths of Night

In the depths of night
With the coldest air
Seeping through all covers,
Gauzy wisps of thoughts
Tantalize insights and
Tickle my mind awake.

Clarity of thought comes
Unhampered by day's bustle
And countless sensations
Clamoring for attention
That squeeze out images,
Metaphors and allusions.

Newly swept clean,
Life's path now glitters
In the soft moonlight.
Flanked by friendly stars
Stretching the curve of space,
I can see clear to Dawn.

Wishing to Be Remembered

I am no Helen Keller
Shining through her darkness;
No Madam Curie piercing
Mysteries of the molecules;
No Eleanor Roosevelt
Connecting peoples and nations.

I am just me.
Even I wish for a legacy,
A continuation with a future past me.
Is that vaingloriousness?

Stillborn

Images from dreams
Seep through rising consciousness
In early morning dimness.

Before eyes open to the waking world,
A mind pause
To remember the night truths revealed.

Held tightly in a mental fist
To save wispy spider silk thoughts
'Till shifting them to concrete words,

This fragile newborn creation
Is assaulted with reality and
Dies before taking a second breath.

A New World

In the middle of the night
I wake to a unique world
Awash with dazzling light.
As the full moon shines, as bright
As midday's hottest light,
Moonbeams bedazzle
All those far below.
I will hold this world tight.

Time's Paradox

Time Is:
Factual/ Felt
Concrete / Abstract
A measure/ A feeling
Linear / Circular
Hard and solid/ Soft and squishy

A moment lasts forever;
A month passes in a flash.
Tomorrow is
October.

Schrodinger's Cat

I know that I'm not now
The me that once I was,
But which of these is me?
Can there be more me's of me
Each as true of me like
Schrodinger's strange cat
Shifting between two Now's?
How many me's are there
Each in their own place
To grow and learn, in time,
How to remember me?
I am the me I was,
I am the me I'm now
And I will still be me
As time flows ever on.
Love and remember me
From all my times with you,
And I will hold you tight
Until the final light.

PART II

I Remember

I remember
Watching my father devolve—
Eaten away from
Research physicist and writer
With clear thoughts and hearty laughs
And piercing eyes who saw my inner self
And valued me as me myself
To become an empty shell, hollow, lost.

His favorite dessert was ice cream.
A night came when I put a bowl in front of him.
Puzzled, he looked at it and looked at me.
I asked, why aren't you eating your ice cream?
His answered pierced me through heart and mind.
"I don't know what to do."

In the Valley of Darkness

I have no other choice,
No alternative
But to walk this path.

My journey thus begins
Triggered from within
To search for meaning.

Still in deepest night
There are moon and stars
Shinning high and bright.

I'm guided from afar
Pointed on my way
To find my future.

Loss is left behind,
And love flows along
Keeping me secure.

We will meet again
Where I'll still be yours
And you will be mine.

Why Birds Sing

Nonnie, why do the birdies sing?
So they can tell us what they see
And where they go.

Nonnie, why do the birdies fly?
So they can find each other
And have freedom.

Nonnie, why do the birdies die?
So they can live forever
With each other.

Home

Cradled in my lover's arms
Safe, secure from all life's harms,
Sheltered there 'til end of time
I am his and he is mine.

Linked together
He to me
And I to him
Stronger both
We'll never part.

My Knight

I grapple with fears,
I wrestle with loss,
I grieve for lost years.
I fear what's to come.

I'm here with my love
Who loves as I was
And loves as I am
And as I will be.

My shield from all fear,
My cool, soothing balm,
My guide through deep swamps
Who keeps me from harm.

We'll travel this road
That we didn't choose
Together we'll face
Whatever will be.

PART III

A Deeper Step Into the Abyss

Two years ago
My world sundered
Into a before
And a now
Of an unknown and dark future.
Short term memory is truncated,
But words are not yet lost.
Words still trip off my tongue with no mental pause.
I can start a task and then hit a pause of
"What do I do next?"
I can start to walk somewhere and hit a pause of
"Where do I go now??"
How many more steps are there
Between
"Where am I??" and "Who am I???"

The Inquisition

I sit in front of the Inquisitor awaiting my fate.
Calmly, dispassionately she quickly reads
The statement that will seal my demise—
A fifty-word story filled with details of Anna
And the calamity that befalls her.

Poor Anna.
I understand every word read:
None outside my mental dictionary.
The words stream into my ears,
Run across the insides of my eyelids,
Spend eon long micro seconds
Trying to press into my brain,
Then evaporate,
Leaving only faint whispers behind.

She asks me to tell her
Details of what happened to Anna.
I know All that happened to Anna.
She fell into the abyss and is lost.

How Fast is Slow?

I am losing it
And
I will lose it all.
How soon,
How steep my decline?

Is the change, now a trickle,
To become a raging torrent
Sweeping away all in its path?
When will I not know that I am gone?

Sharp shards of broken memories
Lay shattered on the floor
Of my waking mind.
Pieces scrambled
Mixing deep past
With possible futures
I do not want to have.

The Unchosen Path

I'm on a path I did not choose nor want.
Here with no reason, no purpose
And no good sacrifice.
Ranting and railing serves no use.

All the ties that bind me with others
Are dissolving, stretching and snapping.
With each lost connection,
I'm less and less me.

The others become gauzy and sheer.
No, not them, it's me disappearing.
I reach out to sense them
And cannot touch them.

Definitions of Fear

Fear
Enters softly
On cat feet;
Or swirls around like fog
On a cold morning
And isolates you.

Fear
Takes
Other faces,
Other personas,
Wears masks
And speaks in tongues.

Fear
Stomps in
With heavy boots
Three sizes too large,
Mud smeared:
Thump, thump, thump.

Fear
Screeches in
High tones like
Nails on
Slate blackboards.

Fear
Growls in
Low pitched tones
Unheard by ears;
Pulses as waves
Through body and soul.

Feelings

Sadness seeps into my heart
And is pumped to every cell
From mind and eye and throat
'Till I'm bathed in loss.

It pools in my feet
And I walk on lost years.
It drips from my fingers
As memories evaporate.

Mental Storm

Fear rumbles over the horizon
With lightning bolts of hot destruction
Burning away mental highways.
Cold hail crushes tender thoughts.

But, sweet winds still push storms away
And warm sun encourages
Tender shoots to sprout.
Light bathes gently across my mind
Coaxing good memories and
Keeping connections.

With knowledge that the day is quickly passing
And the night will be long and dark,
I cherish the remaining light.

Circle of Life

A newborn's eyes have soft focus,
Not sharp or clear.
Sounds hold no meaning, no context:
The world unknown.
But, day by day the baby unfolds
And meaning comes to sight and sound
Until connected to all around
She joins the community of life.
From all unknowing she captures
Connections to time, people and place.
Naming them and making them hers.
She moves forward into the wide world
Conquering language and
Communicating with others
To form relationships
Becoming part of humanity's
Wide web.
But time swiftly flies and
Brings her back to her earliest world
When all was new and unknown:
Sounds heard, but not understood;
Things seen, but not named.
Her very name is lost to her.

A Morbid Gift

Some are taken in a moment
Stepping from life to death
With no time for transition,
But most have time to plan,
To think, to come to closure
Before life ends.
Yet when big Al moves in,
Death is faced long before it comes.
We walk an ever downward sloping path,
Striped of chance to be ourselves until our end
Or plan ahead for what we know will be,
To lessen burdens for those we love,
As we will be lost before we die.

The Disappeared

It has happened before:
Vast multitudes lost,
Destroyed,
Obliterated,
Erased.

Targeted and chosen for destruction:
Dehumanized,
Annihilated,
Extinguished,
Gone.

Stalin's gulags swallowing thousands,
Hitler's ovens burning a generation,
Pol Pot's killing fields,
Atrocities through time,
And it is happening to me.

My very being shaved cell by cell,
Pared away and gone astray,
Connections disconnected;
A hollowing of my essence.

Melting away my past
Like spring sun on winter's snow.
Drop by drop snow transformed to water
That flows away and is gone.

I look inside and cannot find the me who I was,
Where I was and what I was to others.
I have no inner Google to search for answers;
No Webster's open for a million words
To bond with others.

I am an empty gourd with its seeds scooped out.
The wind whistles through me.
My light leaks away.
What am I now to be?

Uneasy Ground

The whole earth shifts and tilts.
It's very texture
Changed from solid stillness
To rippling motion.
Holes appear beneath me.
I spread my feet apart
And open wide my arms
To give stability.
From afar, I must seem
To be a penitent
There waiting to be saved
From some deep tragedy.
What is it that I've done
To bring me thus to here
And leave me all alone
To face what I cannot know.

Hello?...Hello??...

Can anyone now hear me?
Where has everyone gone?
What is this different place?
Can you still see me?
Can you still feel me?
Have I become a gauzy smoke image?
Do your hands pass through me
With no recognition of who I am?
Am I now unseen unheard?
What did I do to merit
Such disregard?
I'm here at the cliff's bottom,
Looking up to where I was.
Is anyone there to hear me?
Is anyone there to see me?
Is no one there to help me?
Where has everyone gone?

Grave Issues

I sense the chill of death
Seeping upwards
From far beneath to ooze along fair earth
And lie at my feet.

Cold swirls round and nestles
The curve of my back.
Ankles and bony knee caps
Are locked in damp chill.

All warmth is extinguished.
Warmth and light is leaving,
As night closes in.

Balancing Act

I step out onto the wire
High above the circus crowd
With just one pole for balance
While all below are watching
And waiting to see me fall.
One foot slides along the wire
Toes gripping for surety.
Will I make it in safety
Over to the other side
Or will I slip and take a fall?
Which ending do they wish for??

Diabolical Rollercoaster

(in my mind)

Sitting in the last car
Of a long line of roller coaster cars
All empty,
Except for me.
No driver ahead,
No one waiting below,
No other rides whirling and twirling;
Just this serpentine monster
That has caught me.
It chugs up the first big hill then
Pitches over in a head rushing descent
With stomach dropping free fall
Plunging to certain catastrophe.
I shout a silent scream,
But no one hears.

Who I Am

I don't want to tell my dreams.
Because,
Then
You would know the pieces of me.
You would look under my bed and see my remnants hidden
there:
....each strand of hair loosed by comb,
....each dead skin cell floated to the floor,
....each fragment of nail clipping flung
past the trashcan,
All gathered under my bed.
Hidden
Just for me to know.
But You
Would take my pieces and make another me from me.
A me not who I am.
I don't want to be another's me,
I want to be the me I am.
So, no one goes inside my head
Nor ever looks beneath my bed.
And I am me what I want to be
With all my pieces just for me.

PART IV

Burdens

We all carry burdens:
Some seen
Some unseen
Some temporary
Some permanent.
Some small enough to fit in a pocket.
Some a fifty-pound sack
Slung over a shoulder
Bending us down.
Some choose to carry them alone.
Some have no choice but to go alone.
Others have support,
Asked for or unasked.
Burdens make and break us.
We are human.

Verdict

So, it has happened,
The word has been spoken
Out loud;
Released into the air
There
For all to see and hear.

Irrefutable.
No longer
Maybe or If
Or even
Probable,

But,
Sits there
In the light
Of knowledge.

Now
All that is left
Is
To live through it.

Concealed/Revealed

Long ago Michelangelo
Looked at a block of marble
And saw a figure there inside
Trapped deep within the uncut stone
Waiting to be released, set free
For all to marvel and adore:
David set free from his prison.
Instead of Michelangelo,
I have a black destructive force
That is tearing asunder my core self
Of who I am, my thoughts, my words
Devolving me to another place
Where I will no longer be me.

Ephemeral Thoughts

As skywriters puff messages from smoke
For those below to see,
That quickly fade or blow away;
Erased with no remains
To give us clues to what has been,
So now my mind is likely bent:
It hears and knows all meaning,
But with a puff of mental breeze
The fragile thoughts dissolve
And drift away.

Stigma

Long ago leprosy's lesions
Were bloody badges of dread disease
Warning others to stay away
Or suffer the same calamity.
Smallpox's markings lifelong
Symbols of fortunate survival.
Polio crippling young and old,
But left self and mind untouched.
All diseases have change factors and burdens.
Most diseases have no stigma attached, no shame.
Cancer is acceptable, can be more easily talked about.
No one knows how to interact with those with Alzheimer's.
Rather, we're scrutinized for missteps, stumbles,
Repeated questions, the story told again.
Those who lose a leg or breast or lung
Are still perceived as who they were
There are many cancer survivors.
No one survives Alzheimer's
And we are lost before we are gone.

Camouflage

Before leaving the house,
I search my mind's closet
For my camouflage outfit
So I can hide in plain sight
In the midst of others.
No netting to hide shape,
No bland shades to blend in;
I wear a verbal mask
Confusing enemies
With mindless babbling talk.
Outward, still engaging
Inward, frantic to hide
And to escape unscathed
My secret still unknown—
I don't know who they are....

Conjoined Twins

Joy and sorrow are conjoined twins
Linked together like Chang and Eng.
Tied together for all of life.

Joy muted with sorrow
Sorrow gentled with joy:
The best of a bad situation.

Joy never complete,
Always tinged or flawed.
Sorrow, never all
If joy can be recalled.

What happens when we
Can no longer remember joy?

The Abandoned House

Down the road a way
There is an old house
Now derelict.

Once it was pristine,
Vibrant, full of life,
Bubbling with interactions,
Connected to neighbors near and far.

Now slumped and fallen in on itself,
Its protected structure punctured
Allows corrosive elements
To eat away its frame.

But hidden tucked inside
Small remnants remain;
Wisps of past wonders
And joys still linger.

Look and Not See

Busy multitaskers
Juggle many jobs
With finger eyes
To pick up what is sought
While real eyes are
Elsewhere bent.
But, now my eyes can look and look,
And yet they still not see.

Space Docking

In this marvelous era,
We have watched in
Wonder of scientific knowledge
That led to exploration of
Worlds beyond our own.
We've seen the slow
Graceful docking of space ships
To space stations in the
Delicate dance to safely lock
Ship to portal allowing
Safe transfers back and forth.
We, too, have myriad inner dockings:
Neurons linking in synapse with others
Transferring information along a
Million cell link
Allowing memories to form,
Ready to be shared when requested
By the conscious mind.
But, nature can go astray
And block the crucial docking.
Information heard and seen
And brought to the docking port,
But not held, left to flicker and float
Off into space of inner mind
Leaving us adrift.

Spools of Time

For most,
The thread of our times
Unspools behind us
Continuously,
Linked unbrokenly
And rewound at will
To reflect and savor
Times and key peoples
In colors still bright
As from long ago.
Some may be tarnished
With blotched faded spots,
Each frame a memory
Still buried in our minds
To warm and comfort us.
Now I am accursed
With parts of crumbled scenes
All scattered through my mind
Disjumbled and unhinged.

Devolving

In day's light
Ev'n the devolving
Can still be seen;
Not yet unseen.

We model
Mohammed Ali
Dipping 'n jiving
To dodge punches.

We conceal
When we do not have
Answers to questions
That others ask.

We allude
When we do not know
What is happening
All around us.

We disguise
When we don't discern
What they are meaning
For us to know.

We infer
The right responses
And mask not knowing
That we don't know.

What happens
When we finally
Cannot be aware
That we are lost?

Lost in Space

Mind is at the center of my being
Filled with data, maps, images,
And thousands of words
To save pasts, explore nows, and build futures.
But here, I have no inner gravity
To hold them fast to me.
They drift and wander,
Pulled by moon and stars.
Then I think that
Time and Space is not fixed
But expands in all directions:
Not lost, not gone,
Just stretched and drawn to infinity.
Then, if I, too, let go
I can sail with my thoughts and dreams
Through all eternity;
Still there in past and futures to be.

ABOUT THE AUTHOR

Margaret Barnes Carter has been a writer and a teacher all of her life. She wrote her first poems when she was ten years old. Writing poems has always been a way of expressing feelings and relationships, a way to make connections with others.

She has a degree in English from Agnes Scott College in Decatur, GA, a Master's in Education from Old Dominion University in 1978 and a Ph.D. in Learning theory from Old Dominion University in 1984. She taught remedial composition, writing and learning to incoming college freshmen at numerous institutions of higher learning in the greater Detroit, Michigan area. She worked eight years at Wayne State School of Medicine, Detroit Michigan helping the faculty learn how to teach and teaching the medical students how to learn the immense amount of information that they were required to learn. Her last eight years before retiring, she was Director of the Holman Learning Center at Eastern Michigan University in Ypsilanti, Michigan.

She is married to Roscoe O. Carter and has three grown children and four grandchildren. In 2015, she was diagnosed with early Alzheimer's. In addition, her father, his mother, his siblings and several cousins have Alzheimer's. These poems were written so those who do not have Alzheimer's can know and feel what it does to us; how this monster destroys us of our memories and our humanity and to prepare and sympathize with those on parallel journeys.

48442984R00038

Made in the USA
Middletown, DE
21 September 2017